You Can't Have It All

You Can't Have It All

Poems

Annis Cassells

By Annis Cassells

‖ Δ ‖

For Rachelle Escamilla —

*Best wishes as you
continue forth in poetry.*

Annis

4·3·2019

Cover photo: Annis Cassells

Author photo: Runa Williams Lemminn

ISBN- 9781796744736

For the loves of my life

Amina, Asila, and Judy

CONTENTS

Late to Madrid

I will go to Madrid
But I will be late.

Too late to see Maria's haunts,
Her special places, beside her.

Too late to recall college days
How we laughed and learned

I will go to Madrid
And trace her spaces

Her apartment
A favorite café

A well-walked *calle*
A well-loved *museo*

I'll remember the photographs
Maria shared, while waiting

Waiting for me
To come to Madrid.

I will go to Madrid
And I will be late.

But not too late.
For our friendship

Had long ago been affirmed
My respect and thanks given

My love spoken
And accepted

By her full-open heart.
I will go to Madrid,

Even though I am late
And Maria is gone.

First Kiss

Fire opal eyes focused,
you sat across the candle-lit table
licked your cheesecaked lips.
And in that moment
I leaned in close
knowing I could not survive
without a taste

Nostalgia

I shimmied into threadbare denim
worn soft as a lady's hanky
And a red shirt embroidered with fish
that once belonged to Kay
the one her daughters gave me, after she died
I wrapped myself in the pashmina
Lynne brought me years ago, before she moved
I scrambled two eggs in butter
like my mama always did
ate from her delicate porcelain plate,
a gift from me one Mother's Day
When nostalgia calls, I surrender.

Visiting Hours

Crowding at the nursery window
fathers, aunts & uncles, grandparents cluck and grin
at a gaggle of first-borns, middle kids and after-thoughts
ravenous, eager to smack at rubber nipples
or suckle at their mothers' breasts.

Crowding at the nursery window
these visitors don't realize how
moments before these angels of torture
pulsed and pressed to breathe air,
pushing grown women into hard labor
arduous as working on a chain gang.
Imprisoned, they strained towards freedom,
rushed headlong into the light.

Crowding at the nursery window,
Look at that head full of curly hair.
There's ours, the cutest one here.
How smart she is already.
He looks just like his daddy.

Crowding at the nursery window,
joy   pride   wonder
Lavish congratulations.
Scant consideration
of those who did all the work.

Sunday Mornings

Sassy curls surge
from crown
to shoulders.

A shiny black bouquet
A nest of Slinkys

A testament to the patience
A bow to the wills

of Black mamas
bound for church.

Inner City Girls Survive

Drought distresses inner city girls.
Oh they have water
take twenty-minute showers
soak hours in claw-footed tubs.
Come summer, they cavort beneath
oscillating lawn sprinklers.

Inner city girls living it survive
a different type of drought.
Reduced by a lack of civility
Controlled by an absence of compassion
Restrained by a want of understanding
Checked in their right to equality.

Civility, Compassion
Understanding, Equality
Commodities in short supply.
All the water in the world
cannot compensate
for societal drought.

Inner city girls living it possess a thirst
A craving that begs to be slaked
Ambition that needs to be fulfilled
Potential that expects to be reached.
By wits and will, and bits of kindness,
inner city girls survive.

Debut

I asked to take canned goods to school
for the poor people,
for Christmas baskets,
my mother said "No.

We are the poor people."

"No, we're not, Mama."

"Poor as church mice."

But somehow she strung together
my Christmas program costume
A plain white blouse
and a long, white skirt
trimmed with gold garland
around the bottom edge
and down one side.
I wore my Sunday shoes,
black patent leather.

She pulled my hair back into a topknot,
formed shiny black sausage curls
that escaped, cascaded to my shoulders.
A wide red bow sat at the crown.

I stood on the Alger School stage
huddled near a boy, now nameless
and faceless with time.
Music tinkled from the polished upright piano
We strained as we started our duet
Irving Berlin's "White Christmas."

8

I remember wincing at the sound of my voice.
Even at seven years old,
I had no illusions
about being a singer.
But there I was on stage
And my mother had made me this skirt,
probably from an old white sheet.

So I sang.

Time Keeper

That round-faced gold Bulova
my grandmother wound each day,
twisting the delicate ribbed stem east of 3.
She watched the hands revolve,
mark minutes in rhythmic ticks.

Passed to me
first granddaughter
nine years old
and counting

Headway

The power of will
Hauled me out of valleys
Depths I never imagined

Propelled me forward
When reluctance reigned
When movement slackened

The power of will
Packed me on its back
Lugged me across the line

First Taste

The Cassells home-place cellar,
earthen-floored,
must-scented, raven-aired.

Grandma Annie Cass-ells
and ten-year-old me,
we heave worn wooden doors,

throw daylight underground,
pick our way down brick slab steps,
stand still, let our eyes adjust.

She leads
bound for thick, unpainted plank shelves
jammed against an uneven patched wall.

She reaches
for a dusty jug
amongst canned pickles, peaches, beets.

She pours
a half-pint jelly jar one-quarter full,
 "grape juice."

She savors
A dark liquid sip
"Ahhhhh."

She passes
the almost-empty vessel
to me.

She cautions
"Just a little now.
Makes you feel warm inside."

She stretches
knobby fingers for the rest
as the jar leaves my lips.

We ascend
hugging peach and pickle jars
Silent glances sealing our secret.

Legacy

Mystified, stunned about the New
York pedestrian mow-down, yet drawn to

Seek out this latest
Tragedy. My tongue, leaden, cannot

Explain what happened, but I'm driven to
Reassure our children about the world

In which they must make a life, a life
Of meaning, a life that embraces

Unswerving goodness, love. I want to
Squeeze them tight

Never let them feel hopelessness
Enable their childhood's rightful

Sweetness, its full-strength trust. Ensure they grow
Strong   Open   Secure

Double Dutch

Thunk, thunk, swoosh

Down in the Valley
Where the green grass grows

Thunk, thunk, swoosh

There sat Sally
Sweet as a rose

Thunk, thunk, swoosh

If I had a nickel
For every time Sally
Sat in the Valley

Thunk, thunk, swoosh

And we kids skipped
Sweet as a rose
'Tween the double ropes

Thunk, thunk, swoosh

Bounced, swerved
Zig-zagged
Left and right

Thunk, thunk, swoosh

The cadence
Our heart beats
Filling the air

Thunk, thunk, swoosh

If I had a nickel
I'd be yours
'Til soda pops

Mama Drove

He always drove, my dad
It was what the man did

So when Mama said
Shall I drive

And he nodded yes
She shrugged a chill

Slick March morning roads
Urged caution, but she drove

Dropped him at the door
In the nick of time

Because not one minute after
She slid into the rigid seat

Beside him and he nodded yes
When she asked

If the doctor
Was in that morning

His eyes rolled upward
Dad lurched forward

Onto the waiting room floor
Right there while she watched

Right there while she watched
Her life spun out of control.

Over slick March morning roads
Mama followed the ambulance

Her own chest lead-heavy
Mouth dry, Mama waited

Until Doctor Whomever
Broke the news, broke her heart

Purse in hand, eyes clear
Mama rose to leave for home

You can't drive yourself, M'am.
The hell I can't.

At the funeral home
Mama's expression, aloof

She only half listened
To the hard-sell pitch

Which one do you like?
None.   I just happen to need one.

Not until Dad left us
Did we kids recognize

The straightness of her spine
The resilience of her spirit

The rock-steady strength
Mama carried inside.

Resilience

I.
The crush comes swiftly
suffocating,
devastating.
In that moment
of fragility,
of vulnerability,
frenzied heart thumps,
pumping blood
to your uncomprehending brain.

The crush lifts slowly.
It just takes time.
Watch for the return of life,
not as you once knew it
but new
and good.

II.
You begin to rise.
And if you can't
yet stand tall
step forward
or feint sideways,
dig into the earth
with one elbow
then the other.
Drag yourself an inch or two ahead
like the downed soldier you are.
Whatever it takes
know you are enough.

Watch for the return of life,
not as you once knew it
but new and good
and worth the effort
Baby steps
or inch-by-inch
it's all forward.

III.

And in that moment
when passion returns,
overruns the heart's hysteria,
overtakes
the clouded-over brain,
you see the light,
the path to acceptance
to peace
within yourself.
You know you are enough
to overcome
whatever comes.

Cancer

Six short weeks

yet a lifetime
Six long weeks
But an instant

The word
Did not double me over
Like a kick in the gut
More like a sibling's
Punch on the shoulder
To claim my attention
The word
Sat just below the surface
Taut, ready
to burst into consciousness
The word
Took command
Spoke aloud
Dig deep, cast wide
Rely on love
Your surgeon's skills
The Grace of the Universe
And positivity
No anti-adversity vaccine
Has yet been devised

Talk

What kinda talk is that
My mother's moon-wide hazel eyes shine
harsh light on my unacceptable grammar

We don't say ain't in this house
It's   That's not right
And   I don't have any

I yearned to please
Learned the code
Knew when not to say Ain't got no

And when to talk proper
Learned double negatives negate
Tacked on the i-n-g's

Precise, equalizing speech
a life-long saleable commodity
Cash language

She talk white
Like a col-lidge gurrl
She think she bettah den us

Commencement

Mortar boards dip then fly
like carrier pigeons.

Straight, military-precise rows
become wiggling masses.

In the stands,
proud parents applaud,
breath-caught, hope-filled,

hearts stinging full,
hands stinging red.

Their children
take flight.

Depth of Memory

Brains
stun me
memories
of a number
Trinity 3-0-1-5-6, our aunt's

The family's favorite, Aunt Gladys
this phone number
imprinted
sixty
years

First
one I
memorized
because crises
could occur. It's best to have a back-up.

In This Century

Forget politics
Gender identity
Forget polarity
And bigotry.
No mother
Can help but shudder
When she hears
San Bernardino
Orlando
Dallas
Paris
Turkey
Belgium
Nice.

A mother's heart flames,
Breath catches,
Brain fires like a rocket.
Where
Is
My
Child?

Even terrorists had moms
who harbored hopes
and dreams for their kids,
that didn't include
being blown to bits on asphalt.

Those moms felt the pain
and joy of childbirth,
worried over bumps and scrapes,

wiped and kissed away salty tears,
shushed and rocked their child.

The same as me.

.

Revelation

It took the birth of my first child
Her weight in my arms firm and dense
Her warm cheek a comfort against my breast
Her tiny fingers grasping mine
Before I understood a parent's pure love
My own parents' pure love

"You did good," my father said
The wide grin on his face matched mine
I'd birthed a daughter, his first grandchild
In the quiet, we both stroked her silken skin
Inhaled her sweet baby scent.

And in that moment I understood
The depth of their love
The sacrifices my parents made
So I might grow and thrive

I Am Sick of Revising This Poem

Sick of adding new names
to the list
Of schools
where kids are killed
Or traumatized for life
Their parents' anguish becoming mine.
I am sick of families
Too soon forgotten
Because it's too soon
To talk about guns.
I am sick of government officials
Sending thoughts and prayers
That fail to staunch the flow
Of assault weapons and blood.
I am sick of mind-controlled
Purse-controlled politicians
Lobbyists, gun dealers and owners
Blaming everything
Blaming everyone
except
The ease of buying guns.
I am sick of Breaking News
That breaks the heart
and soul
of our nation
Sickened by the reality
Of our children hunched in closets

Scrambling beneath tables
"Active shooter" a term
In kindergarteners' lexicon
Sick of watching kids, single file
Hands aloft or cradling their heads,
Gulp a cleansing breath,
As they emerge from
Columbine
Virginia Tech
Sandy Hook
Marysville Pilchuck
Townville
North Park
Stoneman Douglas
And now,
Santa Fe High.

How Could I Know

How could I know
her resolve, her tenacity
How could I know
her perceptive powers,
her sense of the world
and her place in it
I should have
when I beheld
my second-born's face
that August morning at 2:22
when she grabbed the world
and me
her black eyes focused
taking stock
Almost saying Mama

Envision a Mother's Sorrow

The death of a child
of any age
tosses a mother's universe
off its axis

Unfathomable pain
tears her heart,
her mind
every thing

Memories languish,
Linger in torment
Cozy new-baby smell
Chubby cheeks,
Lilting laughter
First words & steps

Her hopes and dreams
Infused his air,
Her vision
To guide him
A cocoon
To encircle him

He grew tall, muscled
Discovered talents
And desires
Devised his plan
His blueprint
No secret

But nothing
No thing
No prayer
Could protect
Her man-child
In mean streets

Dress-Up Box

The sturdy cardboard box
A prized possession
dwelt in the basement
Costumes overflowed
like spring rain run-off

Discarded dresses
Hand-me-down hats
Plenty of purses
Once-shined shoes
Scarves and jewels galore

Two creative sisters
Matched imaginations
Concocted combinations
To fit the personas
They became
And played into life

Ancient Memories

Ancient memories
Beckon, tease
Cast themselves forth
Determined to intrude their
Eloquent entreaties
Force entry
Go against my attempt to forget, they
Hack into the present
Ignore that everything is different now
Justice has lost its purchase, had the wind
Knocked out of it with punches, blows
Led by the enforcers
Masterminded by the spinners
No lawful recourse for
Opening the system, no
Peace
Queries go unanswered
Raised concerns get
Stomped down
Traction of justice skids
Uncontrollably   what's
Vital to restoration, to healing?
Wake and watch
eXamine and act
You   and I   must change the course
Zero in   make ancient memories new

Relocation 1973

Bruised blueberry tears
From windowpane eyes
Darken my breasts
Heart hammers
Stomach somersaults
Brain bellows

What roadblocks will rear up today?
> *Sorry we just rented that apartment*
> *Haven't had time to take down the sign*

> My little brown kids are too young
> My little brown kids are too old

> *You need a bank account*
> *or cash   to get that TV*

Sorry
> *Sorry*
> *Sorry*

What have I done
        moving
here?

These people
    don't know me

don't see me

    don't
       want
    me

Forbidden

I don't recall the days of Jim Crow
or lawful segregation
But I lived in a jewel of a city
Detroit   The Motor City
Where hundreds of thousands
of southern Blacks landed
My Ohio family members included
Fled north during the Great Migration.
They carried their pain, fears
Truths of discrimination
to the new land
Passed them to the next generation
We quaked in the collective memory
Even though we drank
From any water fountain
Went to integrated schools
Sat in the front of the bus
Ate at the Woolworth's counter

Because until we looked for housing
Nothing was forbidden.

Vanished

Morning reveals no scent of you
No Old Spice air descends the stairs
I shake the cornflakes box and toasted snowfall
Echoes against an upturned beehive bowl
Sugar, spoon, milk, and I wait.

But where are you?
The one who shares a young child's
Disgust at soggy cereal
The one who saves the day before it starts

Evaporated like summer's sea water
Vanished before you're forced to wear
A tear-stained denim collar,
Salt crystals dried around its edge.
Before you have to say good-bye.

Discovery

Openings
Where we see to the other side
Like a Chinese garden's leaked scenes
Our focus narrowed
Concentrated

Reflection
In the eyes of another
Someone you love
Someone you hate
Someone you know not

Recognition
Peering through another's eyes
Into her self
Discovering the thing
That makes you sisters

Safe Landing

Weary and soul shrunk
I drop onto a cool gray cement bench
in a barren university hallway.
I run my index finger down
each flimsy newsprint catalog page.
I search for a class, any class
I seek solace, a sense of self,
a sanctuary

Two corridors away
Counseling five-oh-one begins.

I stand on the threshold, scan
the drab, generic classroom,
those staid student desks.
I strain to conjure
an inconspicuous spot,
a space to touch down.
No such thing as a subtle entrance.
It's a counseling class,
desks circled like a wagon train at night.

Two kind-looking women smile, point
to the empty seat between them
the professor says "Come in.
We're getting to know each other."
I sit, listen with half an ear,
sift through shards of myself,
consider what I dare reveal
to this roomful of strangers
what I dare launch
into this unmapped cosmos.

Guest Speaker

Two chestnut brown faces
registered surprise,
eyebrows raised like flags.
One mouth squealed,
"She's a black teacher!"

Two bodies wriggled,
Four eyes sparkled
Four ears hungry
for a voice
that sounded like home.

The Practice

I grasp the edge of the purple yoga mat
recognize the familiar nubbed texture
inhale the rubbery scent.

One practiced motion
unfurls my island.
Marooned for one hour
I feed my body
focus on infinite breaths,
tiny incremental stretches.
Nourish my soul
in silence
chant my mantra.

On this lavender oasis,
sanctuary for introspection,
vessel of reverence,
in soul-to-sole sun salutations
I set my solitary Intention.

Awakening Song

after Sylvia Plath

You're no more your own keeper
Than the hinges that fail to stop the slam
of a rickety screen door

Risk sends you shuddering like an ocean-tossed swimmer.
The idea beckons to your curiosity, and your alleluia
Rings among your musings.

Friends' doubts echo, forge your resolve. I am going.
In a sacred cottage, a rush of rash emotion overshadows
caution. You reserve self-judgment   for awhile

Your eager breath, starved, brushes
her perfect, freckled ear. She waits to listen.
Your raw need seeps from your lips, then spills.

Wordless, she fumbles in darkness
finds her way 'round your scattered limbs.
Your legs open, shy as a novice nun.

Time slows, each second elongates.
And now you sing nearly forgotten notes, long-silent,
rising like the voices of angels.

Homegrown

We relish homegrown tomatoes
Snap peas fresh from the garden
Vitamin rich, full of life and flavor.

We boast of hometown kids making good
Rising eagle-high
Setting the world ablaze.

Neighborhood kids and corn
We nourish   cultivate   protect
Find fertile ground just right for growing

While America's southern border turns toxic
As traumatized children lose their families
In the name of Border Security.

On our watch some grow bitter as quinine
Ripen into homegrown radicals
To someday set the world ablaze.

When Did I Get Old?

When did wrinkles burrow into my skin,
lines furrow my forehead,
fingers refuse to cooperate with brain?

Stealthy, the signs of aging sneaked by
    while I climbed
Climbed rock formations in Utah
the steps of Machu Picchu and Yellow Mountain
into and out of a zodiac in Gallapagos seas

Crafty, creakiness nestled in
    while I rode
Rode my motorcycle along the Snake
through the Rockies and Amish lands
across & through the Chesapeake Bay Bridge and Tunnel

Careless, curvatures arced
    while I stood
Stood before countless students,
on a windy street, for peace
each night at fridge and stove and sink

Erupting, emotions overtook me
    while I cried
Cried over beauty in song, words, sights
at my children's trials, setbacks, triumphs
about love found and lost and found again

Merely breathing, I became old
    facing life
A life rich, jubilant, textured, fulfilled,
scant, hesitant, afraid, hindered,
An ordinary life.   Immune to nothing.

Debris

Former keepsakes
valuables litter indoor spaces
where caked dust lurks in corners
of machine-waxed floors
that meet gray walls

On boulevards and promenades
they fill gutters, lodge in grates
affix to dampened cement
surround street signs and lamp posts
like poppies planted at the base of a tree

Smartphones shattered, crushed underfoot
pages from Grandma's Brag Books
store lists, wallets holding life stories
stray keys, love letters, pocket change

Testaments to lives snatched
mementos remain silent
wait amidst the rubble
to be rescued as hunters search
for their loved ones

It's You

for Judy

Whisper of angel wings
teasing my eyelids open

A tornado that whirls
between shadow and soul

The peak of my Denali
A stream become the Amazon

The fire of Venus's ruby
in my feather garden

Waiting in Mexico

Tedium fizzles
into nothing
no consequence,
no concern

easy-going, bone-tired women
stand on one foot
then the other
in a broken line.

They shift parcels, clutch pesos
Balance stacks of steaming tortillas
on one palm
hablan rapido in hushed tones

I watch, wonder, listen,
speak small words in *español.*
wanting to blend in,
become part of the group.

In Mexico I wait
Without pressing forward
Brow smooth, unfrowned
Grasp fleeting kinship,
Unlike waiting at home.

Games

Pinochle.
Starving college students
seeking cheap fun & a few laughs
You, much too serious

Chess.
Checkmates
In a sterile labor room
As if giving birth weren't enough

Bridge.
Need I say more?
No amount of coaching
Erased chances for censure

Life.
A board game in a box
But my moves summoned me
home to myself

Life Out Loud

The world roared to life
With the gentle placement
Of the long-sought aids
Tawny plastic curved
Behind his freckled ears
The world became a lion

Overwhelming
    Over-the-top
        Overpowering

He'd never heard, never known
Chairs scuffed floors
Flatware clattered on plates
Book pages rustled when flicked
Lips smacked during dinner
Brillo pads screeched on pots and pans

His neck muscles twitched and tensed
With the sizzle of bacon
Plunk of typewriter keys
Squeak of rocking chairs
Blast of car horns in rush hour

Until, teeth clenched,
He couldn't take it any more
Tore loose those offending aids
And like a lucky crapshooter
Tossed them into a drawer,
Shut off life's loudness

Anita Hill in Bakersfield

She took the stage
Humble amid thunderous
Full-house applause
Anita Hill
Urged us to act
Like we are brave
And smart
And know a thing or two
About crushing inequality
And injustice
Urged us to use our voices
Break the culture of silence.
Urged us to speak, insist
Act with our votes
Stand up
Reimagine Equality
"We are not bystanders anymore."

Fair Air

Summer morning ritual
unseal the house
gather chilled dawning air
As if I could store it, harbor it
to fight a Bakersfield afternoon.
As if it would stay, soothe
us when the sun's rays bullet
through double-paned windows.
As if dust motes and particulates
dominant in this toxic air
could be quelled
by a bite or two of coolness.
As if fair air could survive 'til noon.

Alarm disarmed,
its eye once red
like the last barbeque coal,
turns green,
signals accessible doorways,
promises of small cool breezes.
I push back wide vertical blinds,
pull open the leaden slider,
invite the false freshness in.

I glance at the thermometer
mounted on the patio post
look past wooden art-filled fences

beyond neighboring rooftops.
Above the trees
a fresh sun greets me.

In this land of lung-searing summers,
allergens, penetrating dust,
and deadly defoliants,
chilled morning air
dulls memories of discomfort.
I am at home.

Best Friend

for Judy

Her light filters through the cloth of kindness'
Her love, a beacon, draws me near
Lays open my heart
Lights the path to my better self
Her radiance
Her human-ness
My torch

Master Teacher

Miss Holley

Deep, dark eyes, fire-lit coals
set in her shiny brown face
peered over half-frame glasses.
How can you tell
a male tortoise from a female?

Miss Holley waited.
Silence.   Eternity.
The male has long toenails
so he can hold on
during cop-u-la-tion.

Even white teeth flashed
her smile broad, full-lipped.
A few caught on, tittered
while some shot furtive glances,
or sought clarity or looked away.

Day One.
She copped our attention.

Her expectations towered
mountain high
ensuring we could not fail
to outgrow ourselves
to become more.

And Miss Holley was more.
More than my teacher,
she'd lived possibilities
I had dared to imagine.

My dreams
her memories
our faces
reflected in each other.

Tasting Memories

I stand at the edge of the sea
Search for signs of you

The flavor of platinum lingers
Cradled by my tongue
As I remember

Your vibrant laugh now silent
Your skin encircled by this ring

The Gift

My grandmothers' shoulders were broad
Cream-colored, sepia, walnut, and black
Sometimes ridges, like the edges
Of furrows they tilled,
Ribbonned their backs and shoulders
They supported the known world
Like Atlas held up the heavens
They stood proud and strong

On the broad shoulders of these wide-hipped women,
My grandmothers and their grandmothers,
On their convictions
Their work
Their dreams
I stood

Now I'm one of the grandmothers
It's my turn to support the tribe
Be here
Strong, balanced, braced
So on my shoulders
Others can stand

Don't Slice My Bread

Measured segments bore me
The best we can hope for,
a yeast bubble
Or slight deviation in height

Uniformity restrains

Let me gouge boulders
Catch crumbs
Inhale the yeasty aroma
of finger-held fissures
Oozing melted butter.

Let me delight in haphazard hunks
Leave none untried, untested
Skirted or ignored.

Let me taste it all
In its simplicity
In its complexity
Stale or fresh,
Life's staff and stuff.

Anniversaries

Winter 1997
   New December love
   bloomed and reigned
   Amid holiday holly
   and intimate dialog.
   And we became one.

Summer 1998
   July commitment
   signified and celebrated by gold rings
   chosen and exchanged with devotion
   and promises of eternity
   we became one.

Spring 2004
   April vows spoken aloud,
   pledges before dear friends
   at our Wedding in the Orchard
   where, 'til Oregon legislators ruled,
   we became one.

Fall 2008
>October re-wedding
our window of opportunity
as Prop 8's passage loomed.
Before two of our children,
we re-spoke our vows
and beat the vote.
We are one.

My Element

In the old days, if someone inquired,
I'd choose fire
I make things happen, I'd say
Ignite the light within
Incite sizzling patter
For a worthy cause

Today, flowing from the source
Meandering through the course
Is more my style
No torrents, no turbulence
Easy eddies, communication
Awash in understanding

You Can't Have it All

after Barbara Ras

But you can have the wide canvas hammock strung between two trees
like a ship out to sea on your grandparents' hillside.

You can have the giggles of babies, daughters and nieces,
sharing a tub overflowing with toys and bubbles.

You can have Topsail sunrises
and Morro Rock sunsets.

You can speak a foreign language, and sometimes
get the very thing you thought you ordered.

You can't have June and Ward Cleaver,
but you can have your dad wearing only shaving cream and boxers
and your mom wondering what to cook for dinner.

You can have fifty years
of the first day of school.

You can have the Mediterranean breeze
brushing your breasts on a topless beach in Nice.

You can have the hum of a motorcycle and the expanse
of the open road
beckoning you to follow your passion for new places.

And you can have the arms of loved ones
enfold you as you arrive and depart.

You can reconnect with a childhood friend
and feel 45 years dissolve into nothing.

You can have the dream,
the dream of a wooden dance floor in Barcelona,
and you in costume, dancing the Flamenco.

You can have arm-in-arm beach walks, crossword puzzles,
the mist off Niagara Falls, and fireflies in quart jars.

You can have growing old
loving and loved.
And when adulthood fails you and you think that no one cares,
you can still call forth the memory
of that catch in your father's voice, his unexpected expression
of tenderness and love
and when you arrived from school your mother was always
home to listen.

There is the voice you can still summon from your depths;
it will always whisper,
You can't have it all
But there is this.

Acknowledgments

Much gratitude to Matthew Woodman, who asked the right questions, sharpened my thinking about this body of work, and helped me make sense of organizing it.

Love and gratitude to Dennis VanderWerff and Joan Raymond, faithful reviewers, cheerleaders, book-end buddies, and friends who know when and how to toss out a challenge and who supported me at every turn. And special thanks to Dennis for his formatting assistance.

With great appreciation and thanks to my Writers of Kern critique group, The Classics, for their persistence and willingness to learn, read my poems, and give me feedback, even after some said they "didn't get" poetry. Hugs and thanks to Joan Lindsay Kerr, Richard Meeks, Terry Redman, Janet Skibinski, and Ruth Smith.

Thank you to the writing groups, Legacy Writers in Bakersfield and Evergreen Writers in Coos Bay, with whom I've shared some of these poems over the years.

My thanks to Coos Bay besties Karen Blew and Marilyn Wilson, who endured numerous readings under the guise of "after-dinner entertainment."

Much appreciation to Willow Althea, poet and originator of OctPoWriMo, where many of these poems first came to light, and to fellow poets and friends who commented on and cheered those rough beginnings.

Immeasurable thanks and love to my dear family for their encouragement and warm support, my daughters Amina and

Asila, who inspire me every day to try to live up to their belief in me; and siblings Reenié and Thomas, Jan and John.

And profound gratitude to my loving spouse Judy for her kind, thoughtful feedback and wise counsel. Her unwavering support, and unselfish gift of allowing me time to work, were instrumental in making this book become a reality.

‖ Δ ‖

Much gratitude to the editors of the following publications in which these poems or earlier versions of them appeared.

Writing Work: "Visiting Hours" and "Master Teacher" ("Miss Holley, Biology II")
Scarlet Leaf Review: "First Taste," "Relocation 1973," and "Don't Slice My Bread."
Reaching for the Sky: Writers of Kern Anthology 2018: "Resilience" and "The Practice."
Yellow Chair Review: "Talk."
In the Words of Womyn International, 2016 Anthology: "When Did I Get Old?"
Rabid Oak: "Fair Air."

"Late to Madrid" (1st Place) and "In This Century" (Honorable Mention) appeared on the Coos County Historical Society Museum 2018 Writing Contest web page at https://cooshistory.org/oregon-writers-day-winners-announced/

About the Author

Annis Cassells is a poet, teacher, life coach, and freelance writer who lives in Bakersfield, California. She has had articles published in professional journals, local publications, and hobbyist magazines. Her stories and poems have appeared in online journals and print literary magazines, including *Chicken Soup for the Soul: Inspiration for the Young at Heart* and *Scarlet Leaf Review*.

Annis conducts memoir writing classes for senior adults who want to write their life stories for themselves and their families and is a frequent writing workshop facilitator at the Art & Spirituality Center in Bakersfield. She is a member of Writers of Kern, a branch of the California Writers Club.

Her blog, The DayMaker, blends personal experiences and life lessons with inspirational thoughts and coaching ideas. Read it at www.thedaymaker.blogspot.com

Annis was born and raised in Detroit and graduated from Eastern Michigan University. During her 34-year teaching career, she taught in elementary and junior high schools in Ann Arbor and Bakersfield.

Made in the USA
San Bernardino, CA
27 February 2019